INSECT WORLD
LOCUSTS

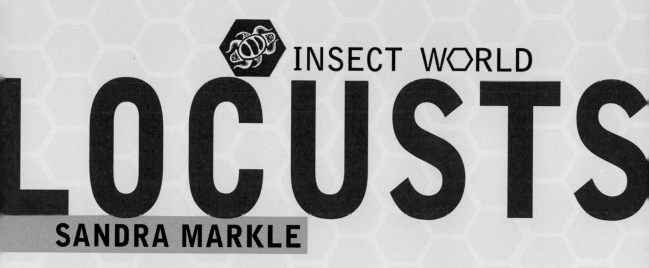

SANDRA MARKLE

INSECTS ON THE MOVE

LERNER PUBLICATIONS COMPANY MINNEAPOLIS

FOR CURIOUS KIDS EVERYWHERE

ACKNOWLEDGMENTS

The author would like to thank Mr. Keith Cressman, Locust Forecasting Officer for the Food and Agriculture Organization of the United Nations (FAO), Rome, Italy; Dr. Allan Showler, Kika de la Garza Subtropical Agricultural Research Center, USDA–ARS, Weslaco, Texas; and Professor Stephen J. Simpson, Department of Biology, University of Sydney, Australia, for sharing their expertise and enthusiasm. The author would also like to thank Dr. Simon Pollard, Curator of Invertebrate Zoology at Canterbury Museum, Christchurch, New Zealand, for his help with the scientific name pronunciation guides. Finally, a special thanks to Skip Jeffery, who shared the effort and joy of creating this book.

Lerner Publications Company
A division of Lerner Publishing Group, Inc.
241 First Avenue North
Minneapolis, MN 55401

Website address: www.lernerbooks.com

Library of Congress Cataloging-in-Publication Data

Markle, Sandra.
    Locusts : insects on the move / by Sandra Markle.
        p.   cm. — (Insect world)
    Includes bibliographical references and index.
     ISBN-13: 978-0-8225-7298-5 (lib. bdg. : alk. paper)
     1. Locusts—Juvenile literature. I. Title.
QL508.A2M13 2008
595.7'27—dc22   2007022288

Manufactured in the United States of America
1 2 3 4 5 6 – DP – 13 12 11 10 09 08

CONTENTS

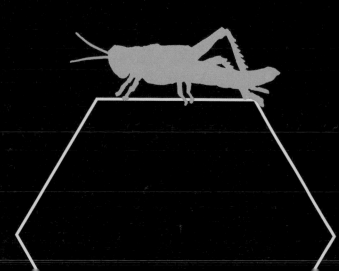

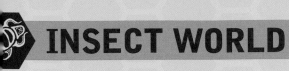

WELCOME TO THE WORLD OF INSECTS—

those animals nicknamed bugs. It truly is the insects' world. Scientists have discovered more than a million different kinds— more than any other kind of animal. And they are everywhere—even on the frozen continent of Antarctica.

So how can you tell if an animal is an insect rather than a relative, such as a pill bug *(below)*? Both locusts and pill bugs belong to a group of animals called arthropods (AR-throh-podz). The animals in this group share some features. They have bodies divided into segments, jointed legs, and a stiff exoskeleton. This is a skeleton on the outside like a suit of armor. But one sure way to tell if an animal is an insect is to count its legs. All adult insects have six legs. They're the only animals in the world with six legs.

This book is about locusts, a kind of grasshopper. When the weather and the food supply change, locusts change the way they look. Then they fly off in huge swarms searching for new places to find food.

LOCUST FACT

Like all insects, a locust's body temperature rises and falls with the temperature around it. They must warm up to be active.

OUTSIDE AND INSIDE

TWO WAYS TO LOOK AND ACT

Some people confuse grasshoppers and locusts. There is one big difference. Grasshoppers always look and act the same way. Locusts can change how they look and behave. A locust can change from its solitary form to its gregarious (gri-GAIR-ee-us) form. Compare the locust's two forms. The solitary form is colored green or brown. This lets locusts blend in and hide among the plants they eat. The gregarious form stands out. Its bright color helps a group of gregarious locusts see one another and stay together. Both forms have big back legs for hopping. A solitary locust's back legs are positioned to let it stay low, so it can creep away and hide. A gregarious locust's back legs make it sit tall so it can look around itself. Both forms have wings. But an adult gregarious locust's wings are longer. They are strong flyers and can fly long distances.

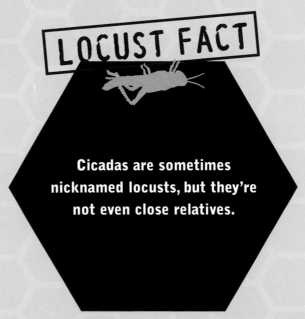

LOCUST FACT

Cicadas are sometimes nicknamed locusts, but they're not even close relatives.

GREGARIOUS

SOLITARY

Take a look at this adult female locust. Its body feels like tough plastic. Instead of having a bony skeleton on the inside the way you do, an insect has an exoskeleton. This hard coat covers its whole body—even its eyes. The exoskeleton is made up of separate plates. These plates are connected by stretchy tissue so that the locust can bend and move. Check out the other key features that all locusts share.

ANTENNA:
This is one of a pair of movable feelers. Hairs on the antennae detect chemicals for taste and smell.

SIMPLE EYES:
These small eyes can only sense light and dark. They help guide locusts while flying.

HEAD

MANDIBLES:
These are hard, toothlike jaws on the outside of the mouth. They are used to bite and grind.

COMPOUND EYES:
What look like big eyes are really hundreds of eye units packed together. These let the insect look in every direction at once.

WINGS: Locusts have two pairs of wings. The first pair is leathery. It shields the lower pair when folded over the back. The wings are attached to the thorax.

LEGS AND FEET: These are used for walking and holding on. Locusts also have taste sensors on their legs and feet. A locust's hind legs hurl it into the air for hopping or to launch its flight. All legs are attached to the thorax.

ABDOMEN

THORAX

SPIRACLES: These holes down the sides of the thorax and abdomen let air into and out of the body for breathing.

OVIPOSITOR: The end of the female's abdomen. It is used for laying eggs.

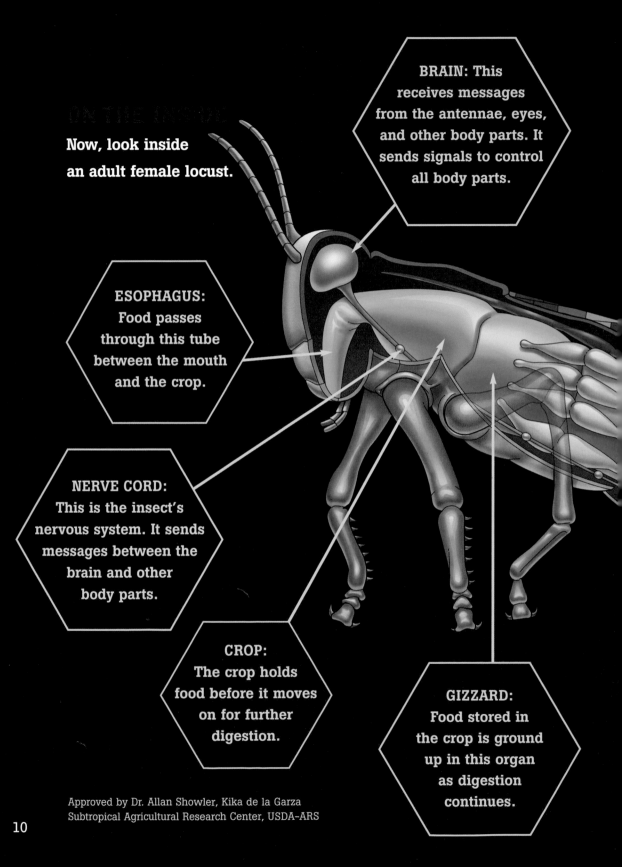

ON THE INSIDE

**Now, look inside
an adult female locust.**

BRAIN: This
receives messages
from the antennae, eyes,
and other body parts. It
sends signals to control
all body parts.

ESOPHAGUS:
Food passes
through this tube
between the mouth
and the crop.

NERVE CORD:
This is the insect's
nervous system. It sends
messages between the
brain and other
body parts.

CROP:
The crop holds
food before it moves
on for further
digestion.

GIZZARD:
Food stored in
the crop is ground
up in this organ
as digestion
continues.

Approved by Dr. Allan Showler, Kika de la Garza
Subtropical Agricultural Research Center, USDA-ARS

HEART:
This muscular tube pumps blood toward the head. Then the blood flows throughout the body.

INTESTINE (GUT):
Digestion is completed here. Food nutrients pass into the body cavity to enter the blood and flow to all body parts.

STOMACH:
Digestion continues here.

OVARY:
This body part produces eggs.

RECTUM:
Wastes collect here and pass out an opening called the anus.

CECA: In these tube-shaped organs, digestive juices are made that help break down food.

MALPIGHIAN TUBULES: These clean the blood and pass wastes to the intestine.

SPERMATHECA:
This sac stores sperm after mating.

BECOMING AN ADULT

Insects grow into adults in two ways: complete metamorphosis (me-teh-MOR-feh-sus) or incomplete metamorphosis. Locusts develop through incomplete metamorphosis. Their life includes three stages: egg, nymph, and adult. The nymphs look and act much like small adults. But they can't reproduce. Compare the locust nymph below to the adult. The nymphs won't be able to fly until they become adults.

> IN COMPLETE METAMORPHOSIS, insects go through four stages: egg, larva, pupa, and adult. Each stage looks and behaves very differently.

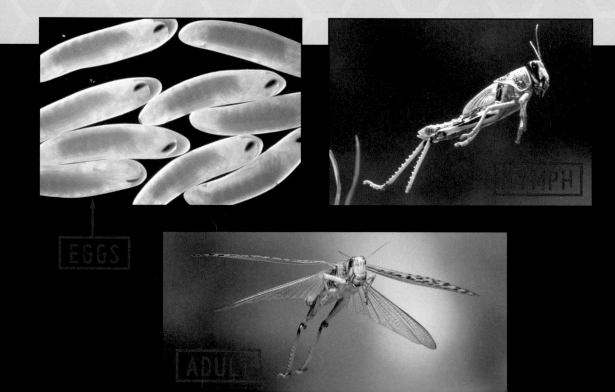

EGGS

NYMPH

ADULT

The focus of a locust's life is eating. Usually a small number of solitary locusts live spread out over a rainless dry area. They move between patches of plants as they eat. When it finally rains, seeds sprout. Plants grow, and there is food everywhere. With the extra food, lots of locusts survive to grow up and reproduce. When the rains stop, the ground dries out again. The food supply shrinks, and the locusts have to crowd together. When this happens, the solitary locusts change to gregarious locusts. Then all the locusts begin to travel in search of food.

When the weather turns dry, solitary-form locusts crowd together to eat the few patches of grass that are left. They can't help bumping into one another. Each bump jiggles the tiny hairs, called setae (SEE-tee), on the locust's big hind legs. These jiggles cause a chemical called serotonin (sehr-eh-TOH-nen) to be released in the insect. Usually solitary locusts move away from one another to be alone. But after a number of bumps and doses of serotonin, they stop trying to escape. The locust nymphs develop more gregarious-form traits too. The nymphs begin to stay together in groups called hopper bands. Once most of the food is gone, these hopper bands march off in search of more food.

LOCUST FACT

Locusts will eat nearly any plant. But they will not touch the leaves of a neem tree. Scientists have taken a chemical from these leaves to spray on other plants, and the locusts leave them alone too.

TRAVELING NYMPHS

With each hop, a locust nymph is able to cover nearly 20 inches (50 centimeters). That's more than ten times its body length.

The nymphs keep hopping until they find food. The ones that reach the food first stop to chew. The others hop on. Soon there are nymphs on the ground and nymphs in the air midhop. The hopper band travels about 1 mile (1.6 kilometers) a day.

All day, the hoppers eat and march. When the sun sinks low in the sky, the air cools. Then the nymphs climb onto plants for the night. When the sun rises, the nymphs climb down. They sit in patches of sunlight to warm up. Then they begin to feed again. Before long, they hop off in search of more food.

As the nymph eats, it grows. Soon its exoskeleton becomes tight. Then the nymph molts, or sheds its armorlike covering. A new coat has formed underneath. This new coat is soft at first. So the nymph must wait for it to harden. Then it starts eating and traveling again. After about 30 days and five or six molts, the nymphs become young adults.

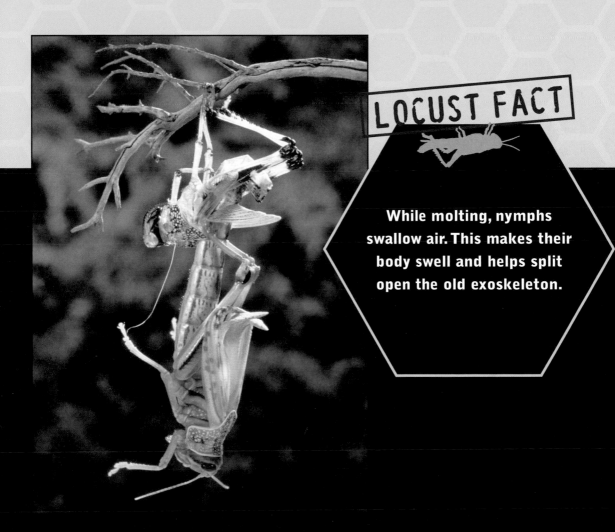

LOCUST FACT

While molting, nymphs swallow air. This makes their body swell and helps split open the old exoskeleton.

EATING TO STAY SAFE

Not every nymph survives to grow up. Predators, like this falcon, catch and eat locusts. But the traveling nymphs get some protection from their food. Gregarious nymphs eat plants, like Egyptian henbane, that solitary nymphs leave alone. These plants contain toxic chemicals. The nymphs don't seem to be bothered by the chemicals. But predators don't like the taste. A predator that eats one gregarious nymph learns to leave others alone. The gregarious nymphs' bright coloring also acts as a warning to predators.

LOCUST FACT

Gregarious locusts may also eat one another. They're especially at risk while molting.

FLEDGLINGS TAKE OFF

Young adult locusts are called fledglings. They have wings, but they are not yet ready for long flights. For four to five days, the young adults take only short flights. This strengthens their flight muscles. They also improve their flying skills. Flying requires flapping all four wings almost constantly. As they become stronger fliers, the locusts reach airspeeds of about 10 feet (3 meters) per second.

LOCUST FACT

Desert locusts give off a scent to keep track of one another as they travel. People say it smells like creosote (KREE-eh-sot), a black, tarry material.

During their first few days as adults, the fledglings also need to build up fat reserves for extra energy. Soon they'll need the energy to fly long distances without stopping. The young adults eat lots of green leaves and grains. In fact, fledglings eat more than nymphs or older adults.

Finally, the adults fly off in search of food. They travel in large groups called swarms. There may be thousands, millions, or even billions of hungry locusts in one swarm. People live in fear of these migrations.

LOCUST FACT

Locusts have taste sensors all over their bodies. They can tell if something they touch is food.

SWARMS OF HUNGRY LOCUSTS

Each locust eats about its own weight of plant matter a day. This is only about 0.07 ounce (2 grams). But when a swarm settles in a field, the thousands of locusts in the swarm each eat that amount. A swarm can strip a farmer's field in a few hours.

When traveling, locusts at the leading edge of the swarm settle to the ground first. Then the others fly on for a bit before settling to feed. Then those that fed first rise into the air and move on again, searching for more food. This way the swarm appears to roll across the field.

There are a number of different kinds of locusts. Some, like migratory locusts and red locusts, eat only grasses or related grains. Desert locusts eat nearly every green plant they find.

LOCUST FACT

A swarm of a million locusts is likely to eat as much food in a day as 20 elephants or 500 people.

Sometimes swarms migrate very long distances. Locusts have been seen flying across the Sahara. Since there's not much to eat in the desert, they keep flying without stopping. Scientists have recorded locusts flying 3,000 miles (4,800 km) without stopping between feeding places. In 1988, swarms of desert locusts traveled a record distance nonstop across the Atlantic Ocean from western Africa to the Caribbean Sea. They flew nearly 3,700 miles (6,000 km).

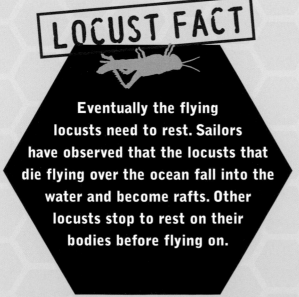

LOCUST FACT

Eventually the flying locusts need to rest. Sailors have observed that the locusts that die flying over the ocean fall into the water and become rafts. Other locusts stop to rest on their bodies before flying on.

TRAVELING FOR GENERATIONS

A locust lives for only three to five months. But swarms may keep on traveling for years. That's possible because the adults mate and produce offspring that continue the migration. With so many locusts close together, it's easy for the males and females to find mates.

LOCUST FACT

Female locusts look very similar to males. But they have an ovipositor, a pointed tail end for depositing eggs. They are also larger. They need to be able to hold all the eggs they produce.

After mating, the locust female probes the soil with the tip of her abdomen. When she finds a soft spot, she makes a hole. In the hole, she lays about 60 eggs inside an egg pod. Then she gives off a frothy liquid that fills the hole. This liquid soon hardens and forms a plug. The plug keeps out ants, beetle larvae, and other egg-eating predators. A gregarious-form female also adds a special chemical to this frothy liquid. This chemical passes through the eggshells. It helps the nymphs growing inside develop gregarious-form traits. The nymphs hatch with the urge to keep traveling.

Locusts in a swarm tend to breed at the same time. Then all the females lay their eggs at nearly the same time. About two weeks later, millions—even billions—of hatchlings burst out of their eggs all at once. They chew their way through the hardened foam plug and crawl out onto the surface. Being one of so many helps the little hatchlings stay safe. Those that survive and are not eaten by hungry predators soon molt for the first time. Then they start to search for food.

LOCUST FACT

Females lay a second pod of eggs about a week later. Some females lay a third pod before they die.

SOLITARY AGAIN

Eventually, the swarm's population decreases. This may happen when the locusts can no longer find enough food and many hatchlings die. Or winds may carry the swarm to places where it is too cold for them to live. Too much rain can drown the young before they hatch. Flooding may kill the hoppers because they are unable to fly away. People also kill the locusts by spraying them with poisonous chemicals. They do this to stop the locusts from eating the food plants they are growing for themselves.

LOCUST FACT

When several generations of swarms have gone on eating farmers' crops, they are called a plague. A plague of locusts may affect a region, many countries, or even several continents.

Once the swarm is small again, the remaining locusts spread out. They return to their solitary lifestyles. They once again hide among plants during the day. At night, they travel only short distances to find more food or a mate. The females lay eggs that develop into solitary-form nymphs. Gregarious nymphs that are still developing change as they molt. They become solitary-form adults.

LOCUST FACT

Solitary-form nymphs tend to be mainly green in the wet season and brown in the dry season. Perhaps those that don't blend in are more often seen and eaten by predators.

Little by little, the solitary locusts travel back to the dry areas. This is likely to take many years. Others that never left their original breeding areas also continue with their solitary lifestyles.

Then the rains come again, seeds sprout, and lots of plants grow. Once again, the locust population booms. When the grasslands start to dry out again, the locusts are forced to crowd together. Solitary-form nymphs change into gregarious-form nymphs. And hopper bands march off in search of food. The locusts have started traveling again.

LOCUSTS AND OTHER INSECT TRAVELERS

LOCUSTS BELONG TO A GROUP, or order, of insects called Orthoptera (or-THOP-ter-ra). That name comes from the Greek words for "straight" and "wing." This group of insects is noted for being good jumpers. It includes crickets, grasshoppers, and locusts.

SCIENTISTS GROUP LIVING and extinct animals with others that are similar. So locusts are classified this way:

Kingdom: Animalia
Phylum: Arthropoda
Class: Insecta
Order: Orthoptera

HELPFUL OR HARMFUL? Locusts are harmful because they eat crops being grown to feed animals and people. But locusts provide food for birds and other animals. In some places, people eat locusts too. In Cambodia, people slice a locust open, insert a peanut, and fry the insect in oil with a dash of salt. In Africa, people eat locusts with honey. Either way, locusts are a crunchy, protein-rich food.

HOW BIG ARE locusts? Adult locusts can be up to 1.9 inches (5 cm) long.

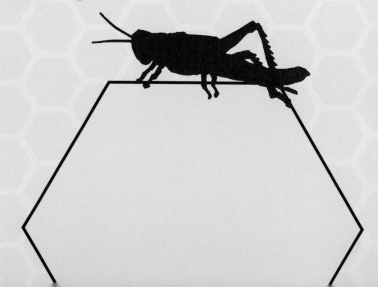

MORE INSECT TRAVELERS

Other insects also travel to find food and better living conditions. Compare these insect travelers to locusts.

Monarch butterflies are unable to survive in cold weather. They fly in flocks, or groups, from Canada and the northern United States to California and Mexico. Some fly more than 2,000 miles (3,200 km) to their winter home. There the butterflies hibernate and rest over the winter. Their heart rate slows down, and they do not eat. As the adults start north again in the spring, they stop to reproduce. Monarchs go through complete metamorphosis. The next generation continues the migration north.

Painted lady butterflies, like other butterflies, go through complete metamorphosis. They can't survive cold weather at any part of their life cycle, so they mostly live in warm places. Butterflies eat nectar from flowers, so painted ladies migrate north to follow their flower food supplies. They migrate into the United States and Canada from Mexico. And they migrate into Europe from southern parts of Africa. Painted ladies only make this migration when they need to find new nectar supplies.

Green darner dragonflies that live in Canada and the United States are usually residents. They breed over the summer and lay eggs in water. Dragonflies go through incomplete metamorphosis. Their nymphs spend the winter underwater. In spring, the nymphs become adults, and the life cycle continues. Other green darners arrive from the south each spring. Green darners eat mosquitoes. They travel north where there are lots of mosquito populations in the summer. Their nymphs become adults in time to migrate south again in early fall.

GLOSSARY

abdomen: the tail end of an insect. It contains the parts for digestion and reproduction.

adult: the final stage of an insect's life cycle

antennae: movable, jointed parts on the insect's head used for sensing

brain: receives messages from the antennae, eyes, and sensory hairs. It sends signals to control all body parts.

ceca (SEE-ka)**:** tubes where digestive juices are made that help break down food

complete metamorphosis: a process of development in which the young looks and behaves very differently from the adult. Stages include egg, larva, pupa, and adult.

compound eyes: eyes that are really hundreds of eye units packed together. These let the insect look in every direction at once.

crop: area of the digestive system where food is held before it is passed on for further digestion

egg: a female reproductive cell; also the name given to the first stage of an insect's life cycle

esophagus (ee-SAH-feh-gus)**:** a tube through which food passes from the mouth to the crop, or stomach

exoskeleton: protective, skeleton-like covering on the outside of the body

fledgling: young adult locust

gizzard: body part where food stored in the crop continues to be ground up

gregarious form: locusts that travel in swarms to seek new food supplies

head: the insect's body part that has the mouth, the brain, and the sensory organs, such as the eyes and the antennae, if there are any

heart: muscular tube that pumps blood

hopper bands: groups of locust nymphs in the gregarious form that hop off together in search of food

incomplete metamorphosis: a process of development in which the young look and behave much like a small adult except that they are unable to reproduce. Stages include egg, nymph, and adult.

intestine (gut): digestion is completed here. Food nutrients pass into the body cavity to enter the blood and flow to all body parts.

larva: the stage between egg and pupa in complete metamorphosis

Malpighian (mal-PEE-gee-an) **tubules:** the organ that cleans the blood and passes wastes to the intestine

mandibles: the grinding mouthparts of an insect

migration: to regularly move from one place to another

molt: the process of an insect shedding its exoskeleton

nerve cord: the nervous system. It sends messages between the brain and other body parts.

nymph: stage between egg and adult in incomplete metamorphosis

ovary (OH-vuh-ree)**:** body part that produces eggs

ovipositor: tail end of the abdomen used to deposit eggs and make an egg case

plague: name given to locust swarms that have gone on for several generations

predator: an animal that is a hunter

prey: an animal that a predator catches to eat

pupa: stage between larva and adult in complete metamorphosis. At this stage, the larva's body structure and systems are completely changed into its adult form.

rectum: part of the digestive system where wastes collect before passing out of the body

serotonin: a chemical produced when solitary-form locusts are crowded. It helps to develop the gregarious form of the locusts.

setae (SEE-tee)**:** tiny hairs on locusts' legs

simple eyes: eyes only able to sense light from dark

solitary form: locusts that live alone

sperm: male reproductive cell

spermatheca (spur-muh-THEE-kuh)**:** sac in female insects that stores sperm after mating

spiracles (SPIR-i-kehlz)**:** holes down the sides of the thorax and abdomen. They let air into and out of the body for breathing.

stomach: the body part that receives food from the gizzard and continues digestion

thorax: the body part between the head and the abdomen

DIGGING DEEPER

To keep on investigating locusts and their relatives, explore these books and online sites.

BOOKS

Kravetz, Jonathan. *Locusts*. New York: PowerKids Press, 2006. Dig into the life of this insect. Learn more about its behavior.

Miller, Sara Swan. *Grasshoppers and Crickets of North America*. New York: Franklin Watts, 2002. Full-color close-up photos introduce these cousins of locusts.

Scholl, Elizabeth J. *Grasshopper*. Farmington Hills, MI: KidHaven Press, 2004. This book investigate the life of this backyard relative of the locust.

WEBSITES

Earth Observatory: Locust!
http://earthobservatory.nasa.gov/Study/Locusts/locusts.html
Discover how scientists are learning to predict when locusts will swarm. This advanced site has photos of locusts and swarms and maps of swarming areas.

Locust Watch
http://www.fao.org/ag/locusts
Check where in the world locusts are swarming. Learn more about how locust plagues are stopped.

One of the Crowd: The Amazing Biology of the Desert Locust
http://www.bbsrc.ac.uk/life/crowd/
Find out facts about locusts. Amazing photos and diagrams let you take a close look at their body parts.

LOCUST ACTIVITIES

MAKE MUSIC THE WAY A LOCUST DOES

This male locust is making noise. Grasshoppers often do this. But male locusts usually only make noise when they are ready to mate with a female. The noise is to warn off other males. To make sounds the way a locust does, find a comb with stiff, sturdy teeth. (Be sure you have an adult's permission to use the comb.) Also collect a piece of corrugated cardboard about as long as your index finger. Stroke the comb's teeth over the bumpy paper as fast as you can and always in the same direction. This noise sounds a lot like locust music. Male locusts have stubby comblike edges on the inside of their hind legs. They make their music by rubbing these edges against the hardened edge on their front wings.

TAKE THE LOCUST TEST

Locusts can jump as far as eighty times their body length. How does your best jump compare? Have an adult partner measure your height. Then mark a starting line. Stand on that line and jump as far as you can. Have your partner mark where you landed. Measure how far you jumped. How does that distance compare to your body length? Your body length, of course, is your height. Don't be surprised if you don't do nearly as well as a locust. That insect's legs are built for long-distance jumps. But then, you don't have to hop to escape being caught by a hungry predator.

INDEX

PHOTO ACKNOWLEDGMENTS

The images in this book are used with the permission of: © Dwight R. Kuhn, p. 4; © Stephen Dalton/Minden Pictures, pp. 5, 12 (bottom), 23; © Steimer/ARCO/naturepl.com, p. 7 (top); © Kim Taylor/naturepl.com, pp. 7 (bottom), 41 (middle); © JEF MEUL/FOTO NATURA/Minden Pictures, pp. 8–9; © Bill Hauser/Independent Picture Service, pp. 10–11; © Nuridsany et Perennou/Photo Researchers, Inc., pp. 12 (top left), 13; © Alastair Shay/Oxford Scientific Films/Photolibrary, p. 12 (top right); © NHPA/HELLIO & VAN INGEN, pp. 15, 29, 35, 37, 38–39; © Satoshi Kuribayashi/Oxford Scientific Films/Photolibrary, p. 16; AP Photo/Alexander Zemlianichenko, p. 17; © MITSUHIKO IMAMORI/Minden Pictures, pp. 18, 25, 27, 31; © Perennou Nurdisany/Photo Researchers, Inc., pp. 19, 30; © Oxford Scientific Films/AUSCAPE, p. 21; © Oxford Scientific Films/Photolibrary, p. 33; © FRANS LANTING/Minden Pictures, p. 41 (top); © Ron Sanford/Photo Researchers, Inc., p. 41 (bottom); © NHPA/IMAGE QUEST 3-D, p. 46.

Front Cover: © Stephen Dalton/Minden Pictures.